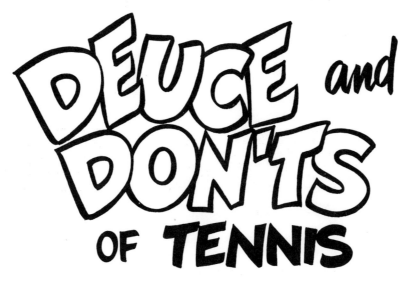

DEUCE and DON'TS OF TENNIS

By Bil Keane

Published by

**O'SULLIVAN
WOODSIDE
& COMPANY**
Phoenix, Arizona

Library of Congress Cataloging in Publication Data

Keane, Bil, 1922-
    Deuce and Don'ts of Tennis.

    Cartoons.
    1. Tennis—Caricatures and cartoons. 2. American
    wit and humor, Pictorial. I. Title.
    NC1429.K2A44   741.5'973   75-14107
    ISBN 0-89019-045-3

FOREWORD
by
Mike
Blanchard

Referee at Forest Hills
Official Umpire, World Championship Tennis

I have read Bil Keane's newspaper cartoons for years and I have played tennis with him. Believe me, he is funnier on the tennis court. He asked me to write something nice in this foreword, but after years of officiating, I am not about to lose my reputation for fairness and honesty. This book will do for tennis what Jack-the-Ripper did for door-to-door salesmen.

However, you will find more laughs here than Wilson has tennis balls. In addition to being a great sport, tennis should be fun. This book of perceptive insight will help make it that way.

Readers ready? Read!

PREFACE

For years I have sat at the drawing board doing my syndicated newspaper cartoons dressed in tennis clothes with my racket at my side. Somebody just might phone and say, "Let's play!" If work starts to interfere with tennis, the work has to go.

My favorite poet is TENNYSon, and of all the United States I like TENNESsee best. I bought some NO FAULT insurance because I thought it would help my serve. At cocktail parties I ask for MIXED DOUBLES and I envy lawyers whose work revolves around the COURT.

Between matches I have managed to compile this book of observations, advice and comments on tennis. It might not improve your game, but I think you will smile more while playing. And, after all, that is the . . .

(Sorry—somebody just phoned and said, "Let's play!")

HOW TO HOLD YOUR RACKET

Right   Wrong

**An important use of the racket
is for deciding who serves first
and who chooses the side.**

Another important use of
the racket is for throwing
when you are burned up.

THE
OVERHEAD

THE
DROP
SHOT

HOW TO CARRY YOUR TENNIS BAG

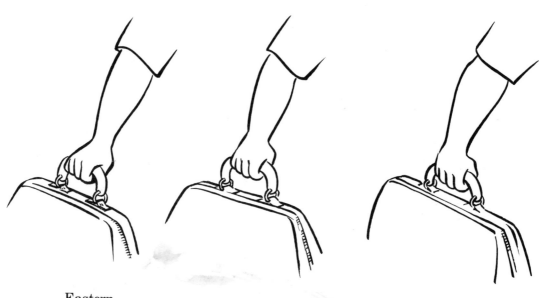

Eastern
grip

Continental

Western

Beginners should seek out
a good pro and listen
carefully to what
he has to say . . .

"I charge ten bucks a lesson."

**Right from the start
tennis will prove to
be excellent exercise.**

"That's it for today. Let's pick 'em up."

"You have something in common with Connors and Laver. You're left-handed."

When you have no one to hit with,
a ball machine or backboard is
excellent for improving your
strokes.

"Nice play — you win!"

When going for an overhead
and being forced to look
directly into the sun it is
always wise to aim at the
ball in the middle.

HOW TO ATTACK THE NET

This should be done only when the net has robbed you of several important points.

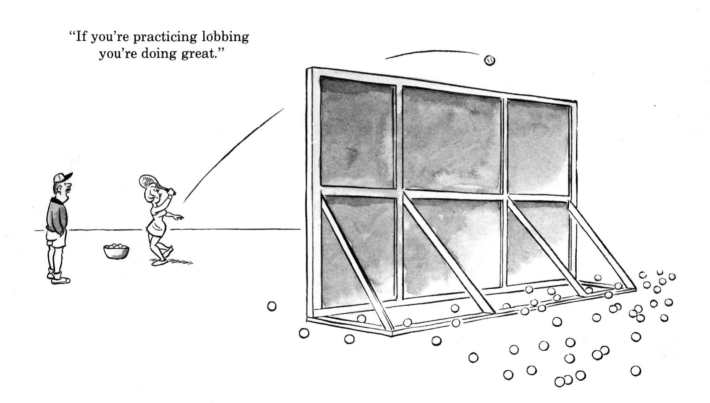

Every player should be familiar with the hand signals and what they mean.

Wait till the plane passes over.

Take a look at the see-through tennis dress on the next court.

The ball was out, but it only bounced this high.

Have I got something for a headache?

Can you give me a lift home after the game?

The confident competitor arrives for a match FULLY EQUIPPED and ready to play.

Pre-game alibis will make your opponent over-confident and give you adequate excuses to fall back on during the match.

"What a party last night! Didn't get into bed till three . . . Got any aspirin, Jim?"

"I can't shake hands — my elbow is killing me!"

"My racket is being restrung so I'm using my
wife's. It's a 4 ½ light—I usually use a
4 ¾ medium."

Some stalling tactics which will help unnerve your opponent . . .

The old "Wait Till I Catch
My Breath" trick.

The untied
shoelace trick.

The old flying
insect trick.

The "Gotta Change Rackets" trick.
(This works best if you own
two rackets).

It is wise to spend some time practicing the calls you will use during the game.

The warmup period is invaluable for getting the feel of your opponent's strokes and sizing up his play.

Basically, there are three kinds of serves . . .

TWIST   **SPIN**   **FLAT**

Most instructors recommend a
back-scratching motion with
the racket while serving.

"Ahh! That feels
GOOD!"

The practice serves exhibited by your opponent may not be his best.

PRACTICE SERVES

FOR REAL

If you touch any part of
the baseline before striking
the ball while serving, it
is a foot fault.

FOOT FAULT

FEET FAULT

ASPHALT
(Very difficult to do
while serving.)

The server should always give the score before serving.

It isn't considered good sportsmanship to continually question your opponent's "out" calls, but sometimes a subtle look will get the message across.

HOW MOST INJURIES OCCUR

Opening the
ball can

Lobbing too short

TENNIS ELBOW is often the result of over-doing it.

(Also tennis HEAD.)

**To prepare your child
for a life of tennis
start him early.**

Teach him the fundamentals—how to hold the racket, how to swing, meet the ball . . . Teach him the simple scoring system.

"Fifteen? Why fifteen? I only won ONE point!"

"Fifteen to nothin' is fifteen-LOVE?"

"After fifteen comes THIRTY?"

"Then FORTY? Why forty?"

"Instead of 'forty-all' I should say 'deuce'. What's a deuce?"

"Tennis is harder than I thought."

"I know all there is to know about tennis
except how to hold the bat."

Most youngsters choose a
professional player to
emulate. By observing a
boy on the court it is easy
to tell who his idol is.

Ilie Nastase

Bobby Riggs

John Newcombe

TIPS TO IMPROVE YOUR GAME

Keep your eye
on the ball.

Bend your knees
on every shot.

Concentrate
at all times.

One of the most important aspects of tennis is concentration. Think only of the game.

"Mommy! Marky's tinkling off the diving board!"

"Could we play a let on that? I wasn't ready."

Most clubs classify players according to their game.

ALMIGHTY BRILLIANT COMICAL DUBIOUS

When the weather is cool, it is a good idea to do your pre-game hitting in a warmup suit, but special care should be taken in removing the suit for the game.

"Oops!"

**You must try to repress
your emotions at all times.**

"NICE SHOT!"

"Double fault! Aw—TOO BAD, John!"

THREE WAYS TO PICK UP A TENNIS BALL

THE RAT-A-TAT-TAT METHOD
Used by the big guys
(pros and A players).

THE FOOT LIFT
Used by B
players.

STOOPID STYLE
Used by the
rest of us.

Tennis need not be an expensive sport—if you work it right.

"I have a new can of balls here . . . let's see . . . now where can they . . . they're right here somewhere . . . hmm . . ."

"You opened yours? Aw, Pat, you shouldn't have done that."

"We can use these if you like. They only
have two sets on them."

"Let's use mine . . . if nobody minds
playing with WHITE balls . . ."

It is a game of endurance. Learn to conserve your energy.

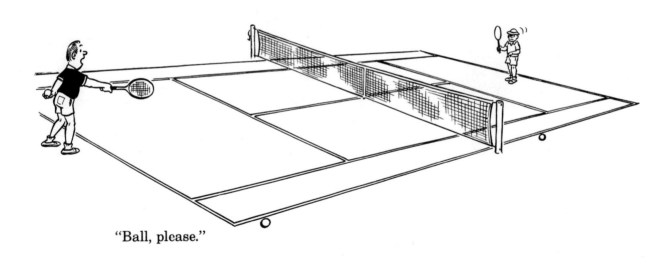

"Ball, please."

"Why the hell did you jump over the net?
It's your ad!"

You will always sleep
well after a good day
of tennis.

**Weather can often be a factor
in determining your strategy.**

"Which do you prefer—the forehand court or the backhand court?"

"Think it's too windy?"

"Okay—you lead five-love,
your serve . . ."

"Aw, too bad—we'll have to
finish this some other time."

When choosing teams in doubles always try to divide up the players evenly in a way that will make the best game for all.

"Jason and I will play you two."

"How are you at very high lobs?"

Mixed doubles is a great social game. Husbands and wives find hours of fun and togetherness playing mixed doubles.

"Here you are, Roger."

"YOURS!"

"MINE!"

"YOURS!"

Men who poach too much
on their female partners
should be slapped. But, ladies,
be sure to use the proper form . . .

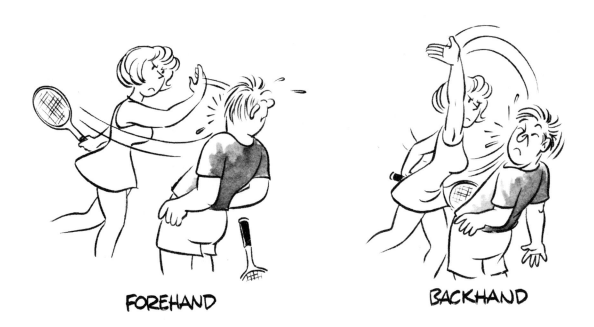

FOREHAND   BACKHAND

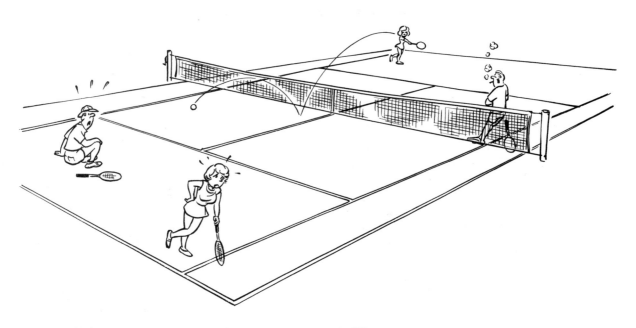

"Her and her damn 'first one in'!"

"Cripes! You don't think I double-faulted on the final point of the tie breaker ON PURPOSE, do you?"

**Old tennis players never die—
they become linesmen and
umpires.**

"I'll be calling the service line
for your match, Jeff."

"Hey! That's great,
Uncle Bob!"

"When will his mommy lift him down out of that high chair?"

"Out."

Many top stars started out as ball boys. Two fundamental skills are required of every ball boy . . .

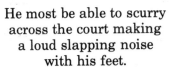

He most be able to scurry across the court making a loud slapping noise with his feet.

He must be able to freeze on the sidelines and dissolve instantaneously into an invisible ball.

By entering tournaments you'll meet new players and sometimes collect a trophy.

"Yipe! Look who I play in the first round—Stan Smith!"

"Howdy! I'm Stanley Smith."

"Mommy, why do we have so many trophies
with lady tennis players on them and
only one with a man on it?"

An 8 game ROUND-ROBIN TOURNAMENT on one court with six teams participating is a great exercise (in PATIENCE).

"Ready, Paul? We're up again in twenty minutes."

The nine-point sudden death tie-breaker has given new life to the game. Be sure each player understands the rules.

"The one who has been serving on that side serves two from over there, then I serve two from over there . . . no, wait . . . I serve two from over here, then Elaine serves . . . or, no, we change sides, then it's three serves for the person on . . . Oh, hell! Let's play it out!"

Television has brought the sport to many people who never before saw a tennis match.

"I believe Arthur Ashe is dealing, but I'm not sure what inning it is."

"I don't care what the rule book says!
Now, according to Bud Collins . . ."

Absolutely the most difficult part of tennis is smiling and shaking hands at the net when you have just been slaughtered.

"Thankyounicegame."

Billie Jean King has
been a strong influence
in bringing women's
lib to the game.

"Thank you, linespersons—
thank you, ballpersons."